Congress. Senate United States.

Standing Rules of the United States Senate in force April 10, 1888

Together With Rules for the Regulation of the Senate Wing of the Capitol

Congress. Senate United States.

Standing Rules of the United States Senate in force April 10, 1888
Together With Rules for the Regulation of the Senate Wing of the Capitol

ISBN/EAN: 9783337155803

Printed in Europe, USA, Canada, Australia, Japan

Cover: Foto ©ninafisch / pixelio.de

More available books at **www.hansebooks.com**

OF THE

UNITED STATES, SENATE

IN FORCE

APRIL 10, 1888,

TOGETHER WITH

RULES FOR THE REGULATION OF THE SENATE WING OF THE CAPITOL.

———◆·◆·◆———

WASHINGTON:
GOVERNMENT PRINTING OFFICE.
1888.

STANDING RULES

CONDUCTING BUSINESS IN THE SENATE OF THE UNITED STATES.

RULE I.

APPOINTMENT OF A SENATOR TO THE CHAIR.

1. In the absence of the Vice-President, the Senate shall choose a President *pro tempore.*

2. In the absence of the Vice-President, and pending the election of a President *pro tempore*, the Secretary of the Senate, or in his absence the Chief Clerk, shall perform the duties of the Chair.

3. The President *pro tempore* shall have the right to name in open Senate, or, if absent, in writing, a Senator to perform the duties of the Chair; but such substitution shall not extend beyond an adjournment, except by unanimous consent.

RULE II.

OATHS, ETC.

The oaths or affirmaticns required by the Constitution and prescribed by law shall be taken and subscribed by each Senator, in open Senate, before entering upon his duties.

137

RULE III.

COMMENCEMENT OF DAILY SESSIONS.

1. The Presiding Officer having taken the chair, and a quorum being present, the Journal of the preceding day shall be read, and any mistake made in the entries corrected. The reading of the Journal shall not be suspended unless by unanimous consent; and when any motion shall be made to amend or correct the same, it shall be deemed a privileged question, and proceeded with until disposed of.

2. A quorum shall consist of a majority of the Senators duly chosen and sworn.

RULE IV.

JOURNAL.

1. The proceedings of the Senate shall be briefly and accurately stated on the Journal. Messages of the President in full; titles of bills and joint resolutions, and such parts as shall be affected by proposed amendments; every vote, and a brief statement of the contents of each petition, memorial, or paper presented to the Senate, shall be entered.

2. The legislative, the executive, the confidential legislative proceedings, and the proceedings when sitting as a Court of Impeachment, shall each be recorded in a separate book.

RULE V.

QUORUM—ABSENT SENATORS MAY BE SENT FOR.

1. No Senator shall absent himself from the service of the Senate without leave.

2. If, at any time during the daily sessions of the Senate, a question shall be raised by any Senator as to the presence of a quorum, the Presiding Officer shall forthwith direct the Secretary to call the

roll and shall announce the result, and these proceedings shall be without debate.

3. Whenever upon such roll-call it shall be ascertained that a quorum is not present, a majority of the Senators present may direct the Sergeant-at-Arms to request, and, when necessary, to compel the attendance of the absent Senators, which order shall be determined without debate; and pending its execution, and until a quorum shall be present, no debate nor motion, except to adjourn, shall be in order.

RULE VI.

PRESENTATION OF CREDENTIALS.

1. The presentation of the credentials of Senators elect and other questions of privilege shall always be in order, except during the reading and correction of the Journal, while a question of order or a motion to adjourn is pending, or while the Senate is dividing; and all questions and motions arising or made upon the presentation of such credentials shall be proceeded with until disposed of.

2. The Secretary shall keep a record of the certificates of election of Senators by entering in a well-bound book kept for that purpose the date of the election, the name of the person elected and the vote given at the election, the date of the certificate, the name of the governor and the secretary of state signing and countersigning the same, and the State from which such Senator is elected.

RULE VII.

MORNING BUSINESS.

1. After the Journal is read, the Presiding Officer shall lay before the Senate, messages from the President, reports and communications from the heads of Departments, and other communications addressed to the Senate; and such bills, joint resolutions, and other messages from the House of Representatives as may remain upon his table from any previous day's session undisposed of. The Presiding Officer shall then call for, in the following order:

"The presentation of petitions and memorials;

"Reports of Standing and Select Committees;

"The introduction of bills and joint resolutions;

"Concurrent and other resolutions;"

all which shall be received and disposed of in such order unless unanimous consent shall be otherwise given.

2. Until the morning business shall have been concluded, and so announced from the chair, or until the hour of one o'clock has arrived, no motion to proceed to the consideration of any bill, resolution, report of a committee, or other subject upon the Calendar shall be entertained by the Presiding Officer, unless by unanimous consent; and if such consent be given the motion shall not be subject to amendment, and shall be decided without debate upon the merits of the subject proposed to be taken up.

3. Every petition or memorial shall be referred, without putting the question, unless objection to such reference is made; in which case all motions for the reception or reference of such petition, memorial, or other paper shall be put in the order in which the same shall be made, and shall not be open to amendment, except to add instructions.

4. ~~Before any petition or memorial shall be received, it shall be signed by the petitioner or memorialist, and a brief statement of its contents made by the Presiding Officer or Senator presenting it.~~ *Every petition or memorial shall be signed by the petitioner or memorialist and have indorsed thereon a brief statement of its contents, and shall be presented and referred without debate.** But no petition or memorial or other paper signed by citizens or subjects of a foreign power shall be received, unless the same be transmitted to the Senate by the President.

5. The Presiding Officer may at any time lay, and it shall be in order at any time for a Senator to move to lay, before the Senate

---

*Adopted March 6, 1888.

any bill or other matter sent to the Senate by the President or the House of Representatives, and any question pending at that time shall be suspended for this purpose. Any motion so made shall be determined without debate.

RULE VIII.

ORDER OF BUSINESS.

At the conclusion of the morning business for each day, unless upon motion the Senate shall at any time otherwise order, the Senate will proceed to the consideration of the Calendar of bills and resolutions, and continue such consideration until 2 o'clock ; and bills and resolutions that are not objected to shall be taken up in their order, and each Senator shall be entitled to speak once and for five minutes only upon any question ; and the objection may be interposed at any stage of the proceedings, but upon motion the Senate may continue such consideration ; and this order shall commence immediately after the call for "concurrent and other resolutions," and shall take precedence of the unfinished business and other special orders. But if the Senate shall proceed with the consideration of any matter notwithstanding an objection, the foregoing provisions touching debate shall not apply.

All motions made before 2 o'clock to proceed to the consideration of any matter shall be determined without debate.

RULE IX.

ORDER OF BUSINESS—Continued.

Immediately after the consideration of cases not objected to upon the Calendar is completed, and not later than 2 o'clock, if there shall be no special orders for that time, the Calendar of General

Orders shall be taken up and proceeded with in its order, beginning with the first subject on the Calendar next after the last subject disposed of in proceeding with the Calendar; and in such case the following motions shall be in order at any time as privileged motions, save as against a motion to adjourn, or to proceed to the consideration of executive business, or questions of privilege, to wit:

First. A motion to proceed to the consideration of an appropriation or revenue bill.

Second. A motion to proceed to the consideration of any other bill on the Calendar, which motion shall not be open to amendment.

Third. A motion to pass over the pending subject, which, if carried, shall have the effect to leave such subject without prejudice in its place on the Calendar.

Fourth. A motion to place such subject at the foot of the Calendar.

Each of the foregoing motions shall be decided without debate, and shall have precedence in the order above named, and may be submitted as in the nature and with all the rights of questions of order.

RULE X.

SPECIAL ORDERS.

1. Any subject may, by a vote of two-thirds of the Senators present, be made a special order; and when the time so fixed for its consideration arrives, the Presiding Officer shall lay it before the Senate unless there be unfinished business of the preceeding day; and if it is not finally disposed of on that day, it shall take its place on the Calendar of Special Orders, in the order of time at which it was made special, unless it shall become by adjournment the unfinished business.

2. When two or more special orders have been made for the same time they shall have precedence according to the order in which they were severally assigned, and that order shall only be changed by direction of the Senate.

And all motions to change such order, or to proceed to the consideration of other business, shall be decided without debate.

RULE XI.

OBJECTION TO READING A PAPER.

When the reading of a paper is called for, and objected to, it shall be determined by a vote of the Senate, without debate.

RULE XII.

VOTING, ETC.

1. When the yeas and nays are ordered, the names of Senators shall be called alphabetically; and each Senator shall, without debate, declare his assent or dissent to the question, unless excused by the Senate; and no Senator shall be permitted to vote after the decision shall have been announced by the Presiding Officer, but may for sufficient reasons, with unanimous consent, change or withdraw his vote. No motion to suspend this rule shall be in order, nor shall the Presiding Officer entertain any request to suspend it by unanimous consent.

2. When a Senator declines to vote on call of his name, he shall be required to assign his reasons therefor, and having assigned them, the Presiding Officer shall submit the question to the Senate: "Shall the Senator, for the reasons assigned by him, be excused from voting?" which shall be decided without debate; and these proceedings shall be had after the roll-call and before the result is announced; and any further proceedings in reference thereto shall be after such announcement.

RULE XIII.

RECONSIDERATION.

1. When a question has been decided by the Senate, any Senator voting with the prevailing side may, on the same day or on either of the next two days of actual session thereafter, move a reconsideration; and if the Senate shall refuse to reconsider, or upon reconsideration shall affirm its first decision, no further motion to reconsider shall be in order unless by unanimous consent. Every motion to reconsider shall be decided by a majority vote,* [without debate] and may be laid on the table without affecting the question in reference to which the same is made, which shall be a final disposition of the motion.

2. When a bill, resolution, report, amendment, order, or message, upon which a vote has been taken, shall have gone out of the possession of the Senate, and been communicated to the House of Representatives, the motion to reconsider shall be accompanied by a motion to request the House to return the same; which last motion shall be acted upon immediately, and without debate, and if determined in the negative, shall be a final disposition of the motion to reconsider.

RULE XIV.

BILLS, JOINT RESOLUTIONS, AND RESOLUTIONS.

1. Whenever a bill or joint resolution shall be offered, its introduction shall, if objected to, be postponed for one day.

2. Every bill and joint resolution shall receive three readings previous to its passage; which readings shall be on three different days, unless the Senate unanimously direct otherwise; and the Presiding Officer shall give notice at each reading whether it be the first, second, or third.

3. No bill or joint resolution shall be committed or amended until it shall have been twice read, after which it may be referred to a

---

* Amendment of June 21, 1886.

committee; bills and joint resolutions introduced on leave, and bills and joint resolutions from the House of Representatives, shall be read once, and may be read twice, on the same day, if not objected to, for reference, but shall not be considered on that day as in Committee of the Whole, nor debated, except for reference, unless by unanimous consent.

4. Every bill and joint resolution reported from a committee, not having previously been read, shall be read once, and twice, if not objected to, on the same day, and placed on the Calendar in the order in which the same may be reported; and every bill and joint resolution introduced on leave, and every bill and joint resolution of the House of Representatives which shall have received a first and second reading without being referred to a committee, shall, if objection be made to further proceeding thereon, be placed on the Calendar.

5. All resolutions shall lie over one day for consideration unless by unanimous consent the Senate shall otherwise direct.

RULE XV.

BILLS—COMMITTEE OF THE WHOLE.

1. All bills and joint resolutions which shall have received two readings shall first be considered by the Senate as in Committee of the Whole, after which they shall be reported to the Senate; and any amendments made in Committee of the Whole shall again be considered by the Senate, after which further amendments may be proposed.

2. When a bill or resolution shall have been ordered to be read a third time, it shall not be in order to propose amendments, unless by unanimous consent, but it shall be in order at any time before the passage of any bill or resolution, to move its commitment; and when the bill or resolution shall again be reported from the committee, it

1774 S M——10

shall be placed on the Calendar, and when again considered by the Senate, it shall be as in Committee of the Whole.

3. Whenever a private bill is under consideration, it shall be in order to move, as a substitute for it, a resolution of the Senate referring the case to the Court of Claims, under the provisions of the act approved March 3, 1883.

RULE XVI.

AMENDMENTS TO APPROPRIATION BILLS.

1. All general appropriation bills shall be referred to the Committee on Appropriations, except bills making appropriations for rivers and harbors, which shall be referred to the Committee on Commerce; and no amendments shall be received to any general appropriation bill, the effect of which will be to increase an appropriation already contained in the bill, or to add a new item of appropriation, unless it be made to carry out the provisions of some existing law, or treaty stipulation, or act, or resolution previously passed by the Senate during that session; or unless the same be moved by direction of a standing or select committee of the Senate, or proposed in pursuance of an estimate of the head of some one of the Departments.

2. All amendments to general appropriation bills moved by direction of a standing or select committee of the Senate, proposing to increase an appropriation already contained in the bill, or to add new items of appropriation, shall, at least one day before they are considered, be referred to the Committee on Appropriations, and when actually proposed to the bill, no amendment proposing to increase the amount stated in such amendment shall be received; in like manner amendments proposing new items of appropriation to river and harbor bills shall, before being considered, be referred to the Committee on Commerce; also amendments to bills establishing post-roads, proposing new post-roads, shall, before being considered, be referred to the Committee on Post-Offices and Post-Roads.

3. No amendment which proposes general legislation shall be received to any general appropriation bill, nor shall any amendment not germane or relevant to the subject-matter contained in the bill be received; nor shall any amendment to any item or clause of such bill be received which does not direçtly relate thereto; and all questions of relevancy of amendments under this rule, when raised, shall be submitted to the Senate and be decided without debate; and any amendment to a general appropriation bill may be laid on the table without prejudice to the bill.

4. No amendment, the object of which is to provide for a private claim, shall be received to any general appropriation bill, unless it be to carry out the provisions of an existing law or a treaty stipulation, which shall be cited on the face of the amendment.

RULE XVII.

AMENDMENT MAY BE LAID ON THE TABLE WITHOUT PREJUDICE TO THE BILL.

When an amendment proposed to any pending measure is laid on the table it shall not carry with it, or prejudice, such measure.

RULE XVIII.

AMENDMENTS—DIVISION OF A QUESTION.

If the question in debate contains several propositions, any Senator may have the same divided, except a motion to strike out and insert, which shall not be divided; but the rejection of a motion to strike out and insert one proposition shall not prevent a motion to strike out and insert a different proposition; nor shall it prevent a motion simply to strike out; nor shall the rejection of a motion to strike out prevent a motion to strike out and insert. But pending a motion to strike out and insert, the part to be stricken out and the part to be inserted shall each be regarded for the purpose of amendment as a question; and motions to amend the part to be stricken out shall have precedence.

RULE XIX.

DEBATE.

1. When a Senator desires to speak he shall rise and address the Presiding Officer, and shall not proceed until he is recognized, and the Presiding Officer shall recognize the Senator who shall first address him. No Senator shall interrupt another Senator in debate without his consent, and to obtain such consent he shall first address the Presiding Officer; and no Senator shall speak more than twice upon any one question in debate on the same day without leave of the Senate; which shall be determined without debate.

2. If any Senator, in speaking or otherwise, transgress the rules of the Senate, the Presiding Officer shall, or any Senator may, call him to order; and when a Senator shall be called to order he shall sit down, and not proceed without leave of the Senate, which, if granted, shall be upon motion that he be allowed to proceed in order; which motion shall be determined without debate.

3. If a Senator be called to order for words spoken in debate, upon the demand of the Senator or of any other Senator the exceptionable words shall be taken down in writing, and read at the table for the information of the Senate.

RULE XX.

QUESTIONS OF ORDER.

1. A question of order may be raised at any stage of the proceedings, except when the Senate is dividing, and, unless submitted to the Senate, shall be decided by the Presiding Officer without debate, subject to an appeal to the Senate; when an appeal is taken any subsequent question of order, which may arise before the decision of such appeal, shall be decided by the Presiding Officer without debate; and every appeal therefrom shall be decided at once, and without debate; and any appeal may be laid on the table without prejudice to the pending proposition, and thereupon shall be held as affirming the decision of the Presiding Officer.

2. The Presiding Officer may submit any question of order for the decision of the Senate.

RULE XXI.

MOTIONS.

1. All motions shall be reduced to writing, if desired by the Presiding Officer or by any Senator, and shall be read before the same shall be debated.

2. Any motion or resolution may be withdrawn or modified by the mover at any time before a decision, amendment, or ordering of the yeas and nays, except a motion to reconsider, which shall not be withdrawn without leave.

RULE XXII.

PRECEDENCE OF MOTIONS.

When a question is pending no motion shall be received but—
To adjourn,
To adjourn to a day certain, or that when the Senate adjourn, it shall be to a day certain,
To take a recess,
To proceed to the consideration of executive business,
To lay on the table,
To postpone indefinitely,

To postpone to a day certain,

To commit,

To amend;

which several motions shall have precedence as they stand arranged;
and the motions relating to adjournment, to take a recess, to proceed
to the consideration of executive business, to lay on the table, shall
be decided without debate.

RULE XXIII.

PREAMBLES.

When a bill or resolution is accompanied by a preamble, the question shall first be put on the bill or resolution and then on the preamble, which may be withdrawn by a mover before an amendment
of the same, or ordering of the yeas and nays; or it may be laid on
the table without prejudice to the bill or resolution, and shall be a
final disposition of such preamble.

RULE XXIV.

APPOINTMENT OF COMMITTEES.

1. In the appointment of the standing committees, the Senate, unless otherwise ordered, shall proceed by ballot to appoint severally
the chairman of each committee, and then, by one ballot, the other
members necessary to complete the same. A majority of the whole
number of votes given shall be necessary to the choice of a chairman
of a standing committee, but a plurality of votes shall elect the other
members thereof. All other committees shall be appointed by ballot,
unless otherwise ordered, and a plurality of votes shall appoint.

2. When a chairman of a committee shall resign or cease to serve
on a committee, and the Presiding Officer be authorized by the Senate to fill the vacancy in such committee, unless specially otherwise
ordered, it shall be only to fill up the number on the committee.

RULE XXV.

STANDING COMMITTEES.

1. The following standing committees shall be appointed at the commencement of each Congress with leave to report by bill or otherwise:

A Committee on Agriculture and Forestry, to consist of nine Senators.

A Committee on Appropriations, to consist of nine Senators.

A Committee to Audit and Control the Contingent Expenses of the Senate, to consist of three Senators, to which shall be referred all resolutions directing the payment of money out of the contingent fund of the Senate, or creating a charge upon the same.

*A Committee on the Census, to consist of nine members.

A Committee on Civil Service and Retrenchment, to consist of nine Senators.

A Committee on Claims, to consist of nine Senators.

A Committee on Coast Defenses, to consist of seven Senators.

†A Committee on Commerce, to consist of eleven Senators.

A Committee on the District of Columbia, to consist of nine Senators.

A Committee on Education and Labor, to consist of nine Senators.

A Committee on Engrossed Bills, to consist of three Senators, which shall examine all bills, amendments, and joint resolutions before they go out of the possession of the Senate.

A Committee on Enrolled Bills, to consist of three Senators, which shall have power to act jointly with the same committee of the House of Representatives, and which, or some one of which, shall examine all bills or joint resolutions which shall have passed both houses, to see that the same are correctly enrolled, and, when signed by the Speaker of the House and President of the Senate, shall forthwith present the same, when they shall have originated in the Senate, to the President of the United States in person, and report the fact and date of such presentation to the Senate.

---

*By resolution of December 12, 1887.

† Membership increased to thirteen for the 49th and 50th Congresses.

A Committee on Epidemic Diseases, to consist of seven Senators.

A Committee to Examine the Several Branches of the Civil Service, to consist of five Senators.

*A Committee on Expenditures of Public Money, to consist of seven Senators, which shall consider such measures tending to economy in public expenditures as shall be referred to it, and conduct all investigations into the expenditure of public money which shall be ordered by the Senate, unless the Senate shall otherwise direct.

A Committee on Finance, to consist of eleven Senators.

†A Committee on Fisheries, to consist of seven Senators, to which shall be referred all matters relating to fish and fisheries.

A Committee on Foreign Relations, to consist of nine Senators.

A Committee on the Improvement of the Mississippi River, to consist of seven Senators.

A Committee on Indian Affairs, to consist of nine Senators.

‡A Committee on Interstate Commerce, to.consist of nine Senators.

A Committee on the Judiciary, to consist of nine Senators.

A Committee on the Library, to consist of three Senators, which shall have power to act jointly with the same committee of the House of Representatives.

†A Committee on Manufactures, to consist of seven Senators.

A Committee on Military Affairs, to consist of nine Senators.

A Committee on Mines and Mining, to consist of seven Senators.

A Committee on Naval Affairs, to consist of nine Senators.

A Committee on Patents, to consist of seven Senators.

A Committee on Pensions, to consist of nine Senators.

A Committee on Post-Offices and Post-Roads, to consist of nine Senators.

A Committee on Printing, to consist of three Senators, which shall have power to act jointly with the same committee of the House of Representatives.

---

* Membership increased to eight for the 50th Congress.

† Membership reduced to five for the 50th Congress.

‡ By resolution of December 12, 1887.

A Committee on Private Land Claims, to consist of five Senators.

A Committee on Privileges and Elections, to consist of nine Senators.

*A Committee on Public Buildings and Grounds, to consist of five Senators, which shall have power to act jointly with the same committee of the House of Representatives.

A Committee on Public Lands, to consist of nine Senators.

†A Committee on Railroads, to consist of eleven Senators.

A Committee on the Revision of the Laws of the United States, to consist of five Senators.

A Committee on Revolutionary Claims, to consist of five Senators.

A Committee on Rules, to consist of five Senators.

A Committee on Territories, to consist of nine Senators.

‡A Committee on Transportation Routes to the Seaboard, to consist of seven Senators.

2. The Committee to Audit and Control the Contingent Expenses of the Senate, on Printing, and on the Library shall continue and have power to act until their successors are appointed.

RULE XXVI.

REFERENCE TO COMMITTEES; MOTIONS TO DISCHARGE, AND REPORTS
OF COMMITTEES TO LIE OVER.

1. When motions are made for reference of a subject to a select committee, or to a standing committee, the question of reference to a standing committee shall be put first; and a motion simply to refer shall not be open to amendment, except to add instructions.

2. All reports of committees and motions to discharge a committee from the consideration of a subject, and all subjects from which a committee shall be discharged, shall lie over one day for consideration, unless by unanimous consent the Senate shall otherwise direct.

RULE XXVII.

REPORTS OF CONFERENCE COMMITTEES.

The presentation of reports of committees of conference shall always be in order, except when the Journal is being read or a

---

*Membership increased to seven for the 49th and 50th Congresses.

†Membership reduced to ten for the 50th Congress.

‡Membership increased to nine for the 49th and 50th Congresses.

question of order or a motion to adjourn is pending, or while the Senate is dividing; and when received, the question of proceeding to the consideration of the report, if raised, shall be immediately put, and shall be determined without debate.

RULE XXVIII.

MESSAGES.

1. Messages from the President of the United States or from the House of Representatives may be received at any stage of proceedings, except while the Senate is dividing, or while the Journal is being read, or while a question of order or a motion to adjourn is pending.

2. Messages shall be sent to the House of Representatives by the Secretary, who shall previously certify the determination of the Senate upon all bills, joint resolutions, and other resolutions which may be communicated to the House, or in which its concurrence may be requested; and the Secretary shall also certify and deliver to the President of the United States all resolutions and other communications which may be directed to him by the Senate.

RULE XXIX.

PRINTING OF PAPERS, ETC.

1. Every motion to print documents, reports, and other matter transmitted by either of the Executive Departments, or to print memorials, petitions, accompanying documents, or any other paper, except bills of the Senate or House of Representatives, resolutions submitted by a Senator, communications from the legislatures or conventions, lawfully called, of the respective States, and motions to print by order of the standing or select committees of the Senate, shall, unless the Senate otherwise order, be referred to the Committee on Printing. When a motion is made to commit with instructions, it shall be in order to add thereto a motion to print.

2. Motions to print additional numbers shall also be referred to the Committee on Printing; and when the committee shall report favorably the report shall be accompanied by an estimate of the probable cost thereof; and when the cost of printing such additional numbers shall exceed the sum of five hundred dollars, the concurrence of the House of Representatives shall be necessary for an order to print the same.

3. Every bill and joint resolution introduced on leave or reported from a committee, and all bills and joint resolutions received from the House of Representatives, and all reports of committees shall be printed, unless, for the dispatch of the business of the Senate, such printing may be dispensed with.

RULE XXX.

WITHDRAWAL OF PAPERS.

1. No memorial or other paper presented to the Senate, except original treaties finally acted upon, shall be withdrawn from its files except by order of the Senate. But when an act may pass for the settlement of any private claim, the Secretary is authorized to transmit to the officer charged with the settlement the papers on file relating to the claim.

2. No memorial or other paper upon which an adverse report has been made shall be withdrawn from the files of the Senate unless copies thereof shall be left in the office of the Secretary.

RULE XXXI.

REFERENCE OF CLAIMS ADVERSELY REPORTED.

Whenever a committee of the Senate, to whom any claim has been referred, reports adversely, and the report is agreed to, it shall not be in order to move to take the papers from the files for the purpose of referring them at a subsequent session, unless the claimant shall present a petition therefor, stating that new evidence has been discovered since the report, and setting forth the substance of such new evidence. *But when there has been no adverse report, it shall be the duty of the Secretary to transmit all such papers to the committee in which such claims are pending.*

RULE XXXII.

BUSINESS CONTINUED FROM SESSION TO SESSION.

At the second or any subsequent session of a Congress, the legislative business of the Senate which remained undetermined at the close of the next preceding session of that Congress shall be resumed and proceeded with in the same manner as if no adjournment of the Senate had taken place; and all papers referred to committees and not reported upon at the close of a session of Congress shall be returned to the office of the Secretary of the Senate, and be retained by him until the next succeeding session of that Congress, when they shall be returned to the several committees to which they had previously been referred.

RULE XXXIII.

PRIVILEGE OF THE FLOOR.

1. No person shall be admitted to the floor of the Senate while in session, except as follows:

The officers of the Senate.

Members of the House of Representatives.   The Sergeant-at-Arms, and the Clerk of the House.

The President of the United States, and his private secretary.

The heads of Departments.

The Commissioner of Agriculture.

Ministers of the United States.

Foreign ministers.

Ex-Presidents and ex-Vice-Presidents of the United States.

---

*Amendment of December 14, 1877.

Ex-Senators and Senators-elect.

Judges of the Supreme Court.

Governors of States and Territories.

General of the Army.

Admiral of the Navy.

The Commissioners of the District of Columbia.

Members of national legislatures of foreign countries.

Private Secretaries of Senators, duly appointed in writing; and the Librarian of Congress, and the Assistant Librarian in charge of the Law Library.

Hon. George Bancroft.

Judges of the Court of Claims.

The Architect of the Capitol.

The Secretary of the Smithsonian Institution.

2. No person shall be admitted to the floor as private secretary of a Senator until the Senator appointing him shall certify in writing to the Sergeant-at-Arms that he is actually employed for the performance of the duties of such secretary, and is engaged in the performance of the same.

RULE XXXIV.

REGULATION OF THE SENATE WING OF THE CAPITOL.

1. The Senate Chamber shall not be granted for any other purpose than for the use of the Senate.

2. It shall be the duty of the Committee on Rules to make all rules and regulations respecting such parts of the Capitol, its passages and galleries, including the restaurant, as are or may be set apart for the use of the Senate and its officers, to be enforced under the direction of the Presiding Officer. They shall, at the opening of each session of Congress, make such regulations respecting the reporters' gallery of the Senate as will confine its occupation to *bona fide* reporters for daily newspapers, assigning not to exceed one seat to each paper.

RULE XXXV.

SESSION WITH CLOSED DOORS.

On a motion made and seconded to close the doors of the Senate, on the discussion of any business which may, in the opinion of a Senator, require secrecy, the Presiding Officer shall direct the galleries to be cleared; and during the discussion of such motion the doors shall remain closed.

RULE XXXVI.

EXECUTIVE SESSIONS.

1. When the President of the United States shall meet the Senate in the Senate Chamber for the consideration of Executive business, he shall have a seat on the right of the Presiding Officer. When the Senate shall be convened by the President of the United States to any other place, the Presiding Officer of the Senate and the Senators shall attend at the place appointed, with the necessary officers of the Senate.

2. When acting upon confidential or Executive business, *unless the same shall be considered in open Executive session,** the Senate Chamber shall be cleared of all persons except the Secretary, the Chief Clerk, the Principal Legislative Clerk, the Executive Clerk, the Minute and Journal Clerk, the Sergeant-at-Arms, the Assistant Doorkeeper, and such other officers as the Presiding Officer shall think necessary; and all such officers shall be sworn to secrecy.

†3. All confidential communications made by the President of the

---

*Adopted March 6, 1888.

† In Executive session, March 21, 1885;

Ordered, That the injunction of secrecy be removed from following report from the Committee on Rules, viz:

The Committee on Rules, to which was referred a question of order raised by the Senator from Maine (Mr. Frye), as to the operation of clause 3, Rule 36, reported that it extends the injunction of secrecy to each step in the consideration of treaties, including the fact of ratification, that no modification of this clause of the rules ought to be made, that the secrecy as to the fact of ratification of a treaty may be of the utmost importance, and ought not to be removed except by order of the Senate, or until it has been made public by proclamation by the President.

United States to the Senate shall be by the Senators and the officers of the Senate kept secret; and all treaties which may be laid before the Senate, and all remarks, votes, and proceedings thereon shall also be kept secret until the Senate shall, by their resolution, take off the injunction of secrecy, *or unless the same shall be considered in open Exccutive session.* *

4. Any Senator or officer of the Senate who shall disclose the secret or confidential business or proceedings of the Senate shall be liable, if a Senator, to suffer expulsion from the body; and if an officer, to dismissal from the service of the Senate, and to punishment for contempt.

RULE XXXVII.

EXECUTIVE SESSION—PROCEEDINGS ON TREATIES.

1. When a treaty shall be laid before the Senate for ratification it shall be read a first time; and no motion in respect to it shall be in order, except to refer it to a committee, or to print it in confidence for the use of the Senate, *to remove the injunction of secrecy,* or to consider *it in open Executive session.* *

When a treaty is reported from a committee with or without amendment, it shall, unless the Senate unanimously otherwise direct, lie one day for consideration; after which it may be read a second time and considered as in Committee of the Whole, when it shall be proceeded with by articles, and the amendments reported by the committee shall be first acted upon, after which other amendments may be proposed; and when through with, the proceedings had as in Committee of the Whole shall be reported to the Senate, when the question shall be, if the treaty be amended, " Will the Senate concur in the amendments made in Committee of the Whole? " And the amendments may be taken separately, or in gross, if no Senator shall object; after which new amendments may be proposed. *At any stage of such proceedings the Senate may remove the injunction of secrecy from the treaty, or proceed with its consideration in open Executive session.* *

---

* Adopted March 6, 1888.

The decisions thus made shall be reduced to the form of a resolution of ratification, with or without amendments, as the case may be; which shall be proposed on a subsequent day, unless, by unanimous consent, the Senate determine otherwise; at which stage no amendment shall be received, unless by unanimous consent.

On the final question to advise and consent to the ratification in the form agreed to, the concurrence of two-thirds of the Senators present shall be necessary to determine it in the affirmative; but all other motions and questions upon a treaty shall be decided by a majority vote, except a motion to postpone indefinitely, which shall be decided by a vote of two-thirds.

2. Treaties transmitted by the President to the Senate for ratification shall be resumed at the second or any subsequent session of the same Congress at the stage in which they were left at the final adjournment of the session at which they were transmitted; but all proceedings on treaties shall terminate with the Congress, and they shall be resumed at the commencement of the next Congress as if no proceedings had previously been had thereon.

3. All treaties concluded with Indian tribes shall be considered and acted upon by the Senate in its open or legislative session, unless the same shall be transmitted by the President to the Senate in confidence; in which case they shall be acted upon with closed doors.

RULE XXXVIII.
EXECUTIVE SESSION—PROCEEDINGS ON NOMINATIONS.

1. When nominations shall be made by the President of the United States to the Senate, they shall, unless otherwise ordered, be referred to appropriate committees; and the final question on every nomination shall be, "Will the Senate advise and consent to this nomination?" which question shall not be put on the same day on which the nomination is received, nor on the day on which it may be reported by a committee, unless by unanimous consent.

2. All information communicated or remarks made by a Senator when acting upon nominations, concerning the character or qualifi-

cations of the person nominated, also all votes upon any nomination, shall be kept secret. If, however, charges shall be made against a person nominated, the committee may, in its discretion, notify such nominee thereof, but the name of the person making such charges shall not be disclosed. The fact that a nomination has been made, or that it has been confirmed or rejected, shall not be regarded as a secret.   .

3. When a nomination is confirmed or rejected, any Senator voting in the majority may move for a reconsideration on the same day on which the vote was taken, or on either of the next two days of actual executive session of the Senate; but if a notification of the confirmation or rejection of a nomination shall have been sent to the President before the expiration of the time within which a motion to reconsider may be made, the motion to reconsider shall be accompanied by a motion to request the President to return such notification to the Senate. Any motion to reconsider the vote on a nomination may be laid on the table without prejudice to the nomination, and shall be a final disposition of such motion.

4. Nominations confirmed or rejected by the Senate shall not be returned by the Secretary to the President until the expiration of the time limited for making a motion to reconsider the same, or while a motion to reconsider is pending, unless otherwise ordered by the Senate.

5. When the Senate shall adjourn or take a recess for more than thirty days, all motions to reconsider a vote upon a nomination which has been confirmed or rejected by the Senate, which shall be pending at the time of taking such adjournment or recess, shall fall; and the Secretary shall return all such nominations to the President as confirmed or rejected by the Senate, as the case may be.

6. Nominations neither confirmed nor rejected during the session at which they are made shall not be acted upon at any succeeding

1774 S M——11

session without being again made to the Senate by the President; and if the Senate shall adjourn or take a recess for more than thirty days, all nominations pending and not finally acted upon at the time of taking such adjournment or recess shall be returned by the Secretary to the President, and shall not again be considered unless they shall again be made to the Senate by the President.

RULE XXXIX.

THE PRESIDENT FURNISHED WITH COPIES OF RECORDS OF EXECUTIVE SESSIONS.

The President of the United States shall, from time to time, be furnished with an authenticated transcript of the executive records of the Senate, but no further extract from the Executive Journal shall be furnished by the Secretary, except by special order of the Senate; and no paper, except original treaties transmitted to the Senate by the President of the United States, and finally acted upon by the Senate, shall be delivered from the office of the Secretary without an order of the Senate for that purpose.

RULE XL.

SUSPENSION AND AMENDMENT OF THE RULES.

No motion to suspend, modify, or amend any rule, or any part thereof, shall be in order, except on one day's notice in writing, specifying precisely the rule or part proposed to be suspended, modified, or amended, and the purpose thereof. Any rule may be suspended without notice by the unanimous consent of the Senate, except as otherwise provided in clause 1, Rule 12.

OATHS REQUIRED BY THE CONSTITUTION AND BY LAW TO BE TAKEN UNDER RULE II.

———————

BY SENATORS.

I, A B, do solemnly swear (or affirm) that I will support the Constitution of the United States.

[June 1, 1789, 1 Stat., 23.

I, A B, do solemnly swear (or affirm) that I will support and defend the Constitution of the United States against all enemies, foreign and domestic; that I will bear true faith and allegiance to the same; that I take this obligation freely, without any mental reservation or purpose of evasion; and that I will well and faithfully discharge the duties of the office on which I am about to enter: So help me God.

[July 11, 1868, 15 Stat., 85.

BY THE SECRETARY.

I, A B, do solemnly swear (or affirm) that I will support the Constitution of the United States.

And in addition to the foregoing he will also take the following:

I, A B, Secretary of the Senate of the United States of America, do solemnly swear (or affirm) that I will truly and faithfully discharge the duties of my said office, to the best of my knowledge and abilities.

[June 1, 1789, 1 Stat., 23.

RULES

FOR THE

REGULATION OF THE SENATE WING OF THE UNITED STATES CAPITOL.

ADOPTED BY THE COMMITTEE ON RULES, MARCH 15, 1884.

RULE I.

SERGEANT-AT-ARMS.

The Sergeant-at-Arms of the Senate, under the direction of the Presiding Officer, shall be the Executive Officer of the body for the enforcement of all rules made by the Committee on Rules, for the regulation of the Senate Wing of the Capitol. The Senate floor shall be at all times under his immediate supervision, and he shall see that the various subordinate officers of his department perform the duties to which they are especially assigned in the rules following.

RULE II.

ASSISTANT DOORKEEPER AND ACTING ASSISTANT DOORKEEPER.

The Assistant Doorkeeper and Acting Assistant Doorkeeper shall be assigned, during the daily sessions of the Senate, to duty upon the Senate floor. They shall see that the Messengers assigned to the doors upon the Senate floor are at their posts, and that the floor and cloak-rooms are cleared of all persons not entitled to their privileges at least five minutes before the opening of daily sessions. In the ab-

175

sence of the Sergeant-at-Arms the duties of his office, so far as they pertain to the enforcement of rules, shall devolve upon the Acting Assistant Doorkeeper.

RULE III.

MESSENGERS ACTING AS ASSISTANT DOORKEEPERS.

The Messengers acting as Assistant Doorkeepers shall be assigned to duties as follows:

One in charge of the gallery doors. It shall be his duty to see that Messengers in charge of gallery doors are at their posts at least five minutes before the opening of daily sessions. When the Senate shall proceed to the consideration of executive business he shall see that Messengers promptly clear their respective galleries, and close the doors, and reopen them when the Senate shall resume its open session, or adjourn.

One in charge of the main door to the Senate Chamber. It shall be his duty also, to see that Messengers assigned to the various Committees of the Senate are at their posts during the meetings of Committees, and keep the Committee-rooms to which they are respectively assigned in proper order.

One in charge of the Sergeant-at-Arms' stores.

RULE IV.

GALLERIES.

The Galleries of the Senate shall be set apart and occupied as follows: The gallery in the rear of the Vice-President's chair shall be set apart for Reporters of daily newspapers. The southern gallery over the main entrance to the Senate Chamber shall be set apart for the use of the Diplomatic Corps, and no person shall be admitted to it excepting the Secretary of State, Foreign Ministers, their families, and suites, and Senators. Cards of admission to said gallery shall be issued, to such persons as are entitled to its privileges, by the Secretary of State. The galleries over the western entrance to the Senate Chamber, and in the northeastern corner of the Chamber, shall be set apart for the use of the families of Senators, of Cabinet Ministers, and of Judges of the Supreme Court of the United States. No other persons shall be admitted to said galleries except upon the card of a Senator. The gallery extending from the eastern reserved gallery to the Diplomatic shall be set apart for the use of ladies, and ladies accompanied by gentlemen. The galleries on either side of the western reserved gallery shall be open to the public. The front seat in the eastern reserved gallery, next adjoining the ladies' gallery, shall be set apart for the use of the President of the United States; and no person shall be admitted to said seat except upon his order.

RULE V.

PRESS GALLERY.

Persons desiring admission to the Press Gallery shall make application for tickets to the Committee on Rules, stating in writing for what paper or papers they are employed to report, and also stating that they are not engaged in the prosecution of claims pending before Congress, and will not become so engaged while allowed admission to said gallery; said applications shall be authenticated in a manner satisfactory to the Standing Committee of Correspondents. Clerks engaged in the Executive Departments of the Government, or persons engaged in other occupations, whose chief support is not derived from newspaper correspondence, shall not be entitled to admission to said gallery; nor shall the wives and families of correspondents be entitled to admission. The Press Gallery, subject to the supervision and control of the Committee on Rules, shall be under the direction of the Standing Committee of Correspondents.

1774 S M——12

RULE VI.

MARBLE ROOM.

The ante room known as the Marble Room is set apart as a retir-ing room for Senators and such persons as they may think proper to invite into the same. During the open sessions of the Senate, it shall be the duty of the Sergeant-at-Arms to see that such occupation of said room is not interfered with by officers of the Senate or other persons.

RULE VII.

CLOAK ROOMS.

No person shall be admitted to the Cloak Rooms adjoining the Senate Chamber excepting such as are entitled to the privileges of the Senate floor under Standing Rule XXXIII.

RULE VIII.

HEATING AND VELTILATING DEPARTMENT.

No person shall be admitted to the Heating and Ventilating De-partment of the Senate wing of the Capitol, except upon a pass from the Sergeant-at-Arms, or unless accompanied by an officer of the Senate.

RULE IX.

BARBER SHOP AND BATH ROOMS.

The Barber Shop, and Bath Rooms connected therewith, shall be reserved exclusively for the use of Senators. The Bath Room in the Heating and Ventilating Department of the Senate wing shall be for the use of officers and employés of the Senate; and no person shall be entitled to its privileges except upon a card from the Sergeant-at-Arms.

RULE X.

SENATE RESTAURANT.

The large private room of the Restaurant shall be reserved exclusively for Senators and their guests.

The small private room shall be reserved exclusively for the use of Senators and Members of the House of Representatives, and such use of the private rooms of the Restaurant shall not be interfered with.

The viands served in the Restaurant shall be of the best quality, and the prices for the same shall not exceed those stated in the printed bills of fare to be previously approved by the Chairman of the Committee on Rules, and said prices shall be subject to modification from time to time as the Chairman of the Committee on Rules may direct.

The Restaurant shall be kept open during the session of the Senate and during such other parts of the year as the Committee on Rules may direct.

The Caterer shall give his personal attention and care to the management of the Restaurant. The equipment for the tables and for the service shall be first-class. No spirituous liquors shall be sold, furnished, or kept in the Restaurant. All parts of the Restaurant, with its kitchen and office, shall be kept scrupulously clean, and all waste and garbage shall be removed daily. The rooms and vaults connected with the Restaurant shall be kept entirely for its use, and shall not be withdrawn from such use for any purpose. The management of the Restaurant and all matters connected therewith shall at all times be subject to such further directions as the Committee on Rules may give.

RULE XI.

CORRIDORS, ETC.

The Corridors and passage-ways of the Senate wing of the Capitol shall be kept open and free from obstructions; and no stands, booths, or counters for the exhibition or sale of any article shall be placed therein.

RULE XII.

PEDDLING, BEGGING, ETC.

Peddling, begging, and the solicitation of book or other subscriptions are strictly forbidden in the Senate wing of the Capitol, and no portion of said wing shall be occupied by signs or other devices for advertising any article whatsoever, excepting such signs as may be necessary to designate the entrances to the Senate Restaurant.

RULE XIII.

ELEVATOR.

Smoking in the elevator of the Senate wing of the Capitol is strictly forbidden.

RULE XIV.

CARDS AND COMMUNICATIONS IN THE MORNING HOUR.

No cards, letters, or other communications, except letters from Senators' families, and official communications, shall be sent to Senators in the Chamber during the daily sessions of the Senate before 2 o'clock p. m., unless Senators shall direct the Messenger at the Reception Room door otherwise.

RULE XV.

CARDS AND COMMUNICATIONS DURING EXECUTIVE SESSIONS.

No cards, letters, or other communications shall be sent to Senators in the Chamber when the Senate is in Executive Session, except cards of Members of the House of Representatives, calls from the Supreme Court of the United States, letters from Senators' families, official communications and telegrams, unless Senators shall direct the Messenger at the main door of the Senate Chamber otherwise.

RULE XVI.

SWEEPING, CLEANING.

All sweeping, cleaning, and dusting of the Senate wing of the Capitol shall be done, as far as practicable, immediately after the adjournment of each day's session of the Senate, and must, in any event, be completed before eight o'clock a. m.

·

INDEX

A.

455

B.

F.

G.

I.

J.

L.

M.

N.

1774 s m——30

O.

P.

R.

S.

T.

U.

V.: